STEAM
IN THE
WESTERN
HIGHLANDS

edited by
JACK KERNAHAN
FOR THE SCOTTISH RAILWAY PRESERVATION SOCIETY

D. BRADFORD BARTON LIMITED

Frontispiece. Two 2-6-0s head a Glasgow (Queen Street) to Mallaig train near Whistlefield in April 1956. The leading locomotive is K1 No.62052. The K1 was a development by A. H. Peppercorn of Thompson's K1/1 *MacCailin Mor*, which was itself a rebuild of Sir Nigel Gresley's K4, introduced to the West Highland line in 1937. No.62052 is piloting K2 No.61786, one of the class transferred from the old Great Northern area to the West Highland, but which was not favoured with a 'Loch' name, like many of her sisters.

[C. Lawson Kerr]

Published by Lomond Books
36 West Shore Road, Granton, Edinburgh EH5 1QD

Printed and bound in Great Britain by BPC Hazell Books Ltd

introduction

There can be few areas in Britain of greater scenic grandeur than the West Highlands of Scotland, and fewer finer sights than a steam locomotive in action. The combination, steam locomotives at work amongst the mountains and lochs of the West Highlands, are the subject of this collection of photographs.

This volume completes a trilogy by The Scottish Railway Preservation Society on the railways of Scotland in the days of steam, the first two volumes covering branch lines and main lines respectively. The principal lines covered in this book could be described as neither, and indeed, until the end of steam, each used a different head-lamp code from the other on passenger trains. Trains on the Callander & Oban carried the code for ordinary passenger trains, while all West Highland trains, even the push-pull service between Arrochar and Craigendoran, considered themselves expresses.

The fascinating histories of the lines covered, the West Highland Railway from Craigendoran to the small fishing village of Mallaig, opposite the Isle of Skye, worked by the North British, and the Callander & Oban, worked by the Caledonian, have been amply told elsewhere. Suffice here to say that they are lines of such individuality that neither Nationalisation nor dieselisation have destroyed the unique atmosphere and character that exist beyond Craigendoran Junction. The full length of the railway to Mallaig is still in use, while the line to Oban is now a long branch west from Crianlarich, the section east to Dunblane having closed in 1965. All that was not essential has gone, the small branches to Banavie Pier and Loch Tay (although neither were historically branches), and the longer branches to Ballachulish and Fort Augustus, having been closed as traffic dwindled in the face of road competition. Comparisons between the West Highland and Callander & Oban are endless and fascinating, and even these two principal branches provide an interesting subject for this study.

Both commenced at the first intermediate station north of a terminus on the parent system by a junction facing away from that terminus, although only in the case of the Ballachulish branch were through trains run, involving a reversal. Both lines were aiming north to an ultimate destination which was never reached—the Ballachulish line for Fort William, while the ultimate hope of the Fort Augustus line was the Highland Railway's stronghold of Inverness. Loch Leven was the barrier to the former's achieving its goal, while railway politics stopped a railway being built throughout the complete length of the Great Glen. Expensive bridges were features of both lines. On the Ballachulish branch these were essential, to cross the Falls of Lora and Loch Creran, while on the Fort Augustus line the cost was incurred in elaborate but unnecessary castellation of the abutments.

Fortunately the main arteries survive and these are visited each year by The Scottish Railway Preservation Society railtours, the relatively low speed dictated by the curves of the lines being ideally suited for the use of the Society's preserved rolling stock, and while it is unlikely that the steam engine will ever again be seen at work in the West Highlands, passengers can still enjoy the magnificent scenery from coaches of the old LNE, LMS, Caledonian, Great North of Scotland, and North British Railways, in addition, the vehicles representing the last two companies having observation ends, providing yet another facility reminiscent of the days of steam.

Trains on these lines are few and far between, and hence photography in this area was not common; very often a day's journey might result in only one or two photographs, particularly if the desired location was at a distance from any station. This book could not have been produced but for the photographic excursions made in the twenty-five years prior to the end of steam by Campbell Lawson Kerr, who sadly died during its preparation, and to whose memory this volume is dedicated. A lifelong admirer of the steam engine, and its counterpart on the coastal waters around Scotland, he turned his photographic talents to the West Highland following the withdrawal of the old Highland Railway locomotives, although he did not neglect other areas, as has been seen from his contributions to the two previous volumes. Thanks are also due to W. A. C. Smith and W. S. Sellar for additional contributions.

The growl of the diesel is now heard resounding in the hills and glens, but it is hoped that this book will bring back memories, and record for posterity the glorious days of 'Glens', 'Lochs', 'Black Fives' and B1s.

Stornoway, Isle of Lewis   Jack Kernahan

The commencement of the West Highland Railway at Craigendoran Junction. Class 5 No.45214 and D11 4-4-0 No.62681 *Captain Craigengelt* take the West Highland line with the 3.46 p.m. from Glasgow to Mallaig on a sunny day in July 1953. The D11s were introduced to Scotland by the L N E R in 1924, as a development of the design first seen on the Great Central Railway in 1920, but were not normally associated with the West Highland. [C. Lawson Kerr]

Two of the BR Standard Class 5 4-6-0s, Nos.73077 and 73078, were allocated to Eastfield shed at Glasgow, and worked for several years on the West Highland. Here No.73078 is piloting LMS Class 5 4-6-0 No.44977 with the 1 p.m. from Mallaig on 14 September 1955, photographed coasting round the curve to Craigendoran.

[W. A. C. Smith]

The two V4 2-6-2s introduced by Gresley in 1941 were intended for use on the West Highland, but as they had difficulty keeping time over the section between Glasgow and Craigendoran, they were very rarely seen on the line for which they were built. No.61701 is seen here, however, with a northbound train at Helensburgh Upper. The roof provided over the entrance to the station was not a normal practice on the West Highland, and may reflect the influence which the wealthier inhabitants of this area had on the railway company. Note also the concrete signal box, opened in 1941 when the crossing loop was lengthened to accommodate wartime trains to Faslane. Several of these concrete structures appeared during the war on the line, but none is now in use.

[R. J. Buckley]

In the early days of the West Highland, NBR Drummond Class C 0-6-0 No.555 pauses at Row, which was an unusual design for a station on the southern section of the West Highland, having two platforms. All other stations south of Tulloch were island platforms. Note the unusual access to the signal box direct from the footbridge. The station was re-named Rhu in 1924 and closed in 1964, although it had also been closed between 1956 and 1960, operating as an unstaffed halt for its final four years.
[C. Lawson Kerr collection]

Three of the Reid C15 4-4-2Ts, Nos.67460, 67474 and 67475, were fitted for working the push-pull service between Craigendoran and Arrochar. No.67474 is seen here ready to push the 6.12 p.m. from Craigendoran north from Shandon on 8 May 1959. This was one of the five stations closed on 14 June 1964 when the service was withdrawn, and it has now been demolished. Note the typical West Highland signal box, which contained only the levers, the tablet instruments being housed in the station buildings.

[W. A. C. Smith]

station with a much less chequered history than Rhu was Faslane Platform, opened in 1945, and long osed by 1958, when this photograph was taken of LMS Class 5 No.44967 on the 3.46 p.m. from lasgow. A branch from this point was opened in 1941 to serve the naval depot built on the east coast of e Gare Loch, and is still in use in connection with the shipbreaking yard now established on the site of e naval depot. The halt was used by prisoners-of-war who worked on the construction of the Loch Sloy ydro-electric scheme.

[C. Lawson Kerr]

The Stanier 'Black Five' 4-6-0s were regularly in use on the West Highland after Nationalisation. No.44702 is seen here heading north with the 3.46 p.m. from Glasgow near Whistlefield in July 1954.   [C. Lawson Kerr]

eid C15 4-4-2T No.67474 near Shandon with a southbound push-pull from Arrochar to Craigendoran in Jly 1958. This service, latterly operated by a diesel railbus, was designed to provide a greater frequency f service over the southern section of the West Highland and, by providing a connection into trains at raigendoran, to develop the area as a dormitory of Glasgow.   [C. Lawson Kerr]

Peppercorn K1 2-6-0 No.62012 piloting Thompson B1 4-6-0 No.61344 with a southbound train near Whistlefield in March 1957.

[C. Lawson Kerr]

The West Highland, unfortunately, does not always enjoy fine weather, and 28 January 1961 was a day of inclement conditions when LMS Class 5 No.44975 was photographed with a down mixed freight between Whistlefield and Glen Douglas.

[W. A. C. Smith]

One of Reid's Superheated Class S (later LNER Class J37) near Whistlefield on a fine day in July 1941. The mountain in the background is Ben Vane (2328').

[C. Lawson Kerr]

13

For many years Reid's 'Glen' class (LNER Class D34) 4-4-0s were associated with the West Highland. Some heavy trains were worked over the line during the Second World War, and these two 'Glens', Nos.9242 *Glen Mamie* and 9258 *Glen Roy,* were looking worn-out in September 1941 when they were photographed near Finnart, above Loch Long. [C. Lawson Kerr]

Photographed at the same location near Glen Douglas in 1944, War Department 2-8-0 No.77206 and (below) a year earlier, Reid NBR 4-4-2T No.9135 with a Craigendoran-Arrochar local. The only common factor between these two locomotives was probably the Westinghouse pump. [C. Lawson Kerr]

B1 No.61197 piloting Gresley K2 No.61789 *Loch Laidon* with a southbound train out of Glen Douglas. The crossing loop, between Garelochhead and Arrochar, is still in use but the platform was closed in 1964.

[C. Lawson Kerr]

Only a few of the K1 2-6-0s, introduced by A. H. Peppercorn in 1949, were associated with the West Highland, although the design was based on Gresley's K4 introduced specifically for the West Highland in 1937. K1 No.62033 was photographed in September 1949, when new, climbing Glen Douglas bank, high above Loch Long.

[C. Lawson Kerr]

17

B1 No.61344 and K2 No.61792, one of the K2s not named after a loch, head south out of Arrochar and Tarbet station in May 1952. The Arrochar down distant signal, one of the many NBR signals which have all now disappeared from the line, can be seen near the rear of the train.

[C. Lawson Kerr]

C15 4-4-2T No.67474 leaving Arrochar and Tarbet station with a push-pull local in July 1958. Although the train will call at all stations on its leisurely journey, it carries express headlamps, in common with all West Highland passenger trains. This station serves Arrochar at the head of Loch Long as well as Tarbet on Loch Lomond.   [C. Lawson Kerr]

year later at the same location LMS Class 5 No.45400 and B1 No.61396 head south ith a Mallaig-Glasgow train.

K2 2-6-0 No.61772 *Loch Lochy* had received its new British Railways number, but retained LNER apple green livery, and initials on the tender, some twenty months after Nationalisation, when this photograph was taken near Arrochar.   [C. Lawson Kerr]

Two B1s, Nos.61344 and 61197, head south near Inveruglas with a heavy train in June 1951. Even with locomotives as powerful as the Class 5s, both LMS and LNE, trains were so heavy that double heading was the rule rather than the exception, particularly in the summer months.   [C. Lawson Kerr]

The line runs for the eight miles between Arrochar and Ardlui along the west bank of Loch Lomond, but extensive views of the loch are obscured by trees for much of the journey, and a trip on the line in winter, when the trees are bare, can be more rewarding than one in summer; K2 No.61764 *Loch Arkaig* heads a southbound fish train from Mallaig near Inveruglas. [C. Lawson Kerr]

The scenic beauty of the West Highland was marred at a few locations by industry, as evidenced by this photograph of the sidings and crossing loop established at Inveruglas in 1945 for the construction of the Loch Sloy hydro-electric scheme. K2 No.61791 *Loch Laggan* pauses at Inveruglas with a southbound goods in June 1953. Loch Sloy, a narrow and gloomy water surrounded by steep mountains, lies some three miles west of the line at this point.

[C. Lawson Kerr]

The waters of Loch
Lomond, the largest
inland lake in Scotland,
can be seen behind
these two K2 2-6-0s
(Nos.61790,
appropriately named
Loch Lomond, and
61794 *Loch Oich*),
photographed north of
Inveruglas with the
3.46 p.m. from
Glasgow on 5 August
1951.
    [C. Lawson Kerr]

Loch Lomond narrows near Ardlui, and is partly visible in the background of this photograph of Stanier Class 5 No.45214 and Thompson B1 No.61243 heading a train from Mallaig in the summer of 1954.
[C. Lawson Kerr]

he prototype K1 2-6-0—rebuilt from Class K4 by Edward Thompson in 1945—
o.61997 *MacCailin Mor,* with a fish train near Inveruglas in May 1951. [C. Lawson Kerr]

MacCailin Mor, K1 No.61997, photographed among the trees south of Ardlui with the morning Mallaig-Glasgow train in July 1953. The modern vehicle behind the engine contrasts with the Gresley coach behind it, both in the red and cream livery of the period.　　　　　　　　　　　　　　　　　　　　　　　　　　　[C. Lawson Kerr]

In May 1959 two of the few remaining NBR 'Glen' 4-4-0s, Nos.62496 *Glen Loy* and 62471 *Glen Falloch*, revisited haunts once familiar to them and many of their sisters before they were replaced by the K2s in the 1930s. This was for the purposes of a television film and the duo are seen here leaving Ardlui.　　　　[C. Lawson Kerr]

Ardlui station in 1960 with Standard Class 5 4-6-0 No.73078 piloting LMS Class 5
No.44977, waiting to cross an up train. The station building at Ardlui was demolished in
1970 due to subsidence.   [C. Lawson Kerr]

The down starting signal at Ardlui was still an NBR lower quadrant in July 1956. K2 2-6-0 No.61774 *Loch Garry* is waiting for this signal to allow it to proceed with the 3 p.m. from Glasgow, while Stanier Class 5 No.44957 enters the loop with the 12.30 p.m. from Mallaig to Glasgow (Queen Street, Low Level). [W. A. C. Smith]

Two K2s hard at work with a well-loaded 3.46 p.m. from Glasgow, leaving Ardlui in September 1951, No.61794 *Loch Oich* pilots un-named No.61792. Despite the fact that the K2s did not have splashers above the driving wheels, they were provided with splasher type nameplates, although B1s and K4s had straight nameplates attached to the side of the smokebox. Note the height of the up home signal, required to give a background clear of the trees.

[C. Lawson Kerr]

32

Two immaculate 'Black Fives', Nos.45400 and 45214, haul a heavy train out of Ardlui in June 1954. Ardlui lies at the head of Loch Lomond, and until the closure of the pier was the station used by passengers making a circular tour, out by rail and returning by the loch paddle steamer. Similar connections were available at Arrochar and Tarbet, but the piers at Arrochar on Loch Long and Tarbet on Loch Lomond are now also closed.

[C. Lawson Kerr]

The 3.46 p.m. from Glasgow to Mallaig was, like the 6 a.m., a train which ran at more or less the same time during almost all the days of steam on the West Highland. Class 5 4-6-0s Nos.73077 and 44995 are seen here leaving Ardlui with the 3.46 p.m. in the summer of 1955.   [C. Lawson Kerr]

Stanier Class 5 No.45400 climbing Glen Falloch with a Glasgow - Mallaig express in May 1953. The train is loaded to only six coaches, and double-heading, a common feature in the busier months of the summer is not required.

[C. Lawson Kerr

Two views of Thompson B1 4-6-0s heading south down the 1 in 65 gradient in Glen Falloch between Crianlarich and Ardlui in June 1948, six months after Nationalisation. No.1197 retains its last LNER number, but No.61324 (below) has received its new British Railways number.

[C. Lawson Kerr]

The noise of the waters of the River Falloch descending Glen Falloch were christened the 'Vale of Awful Sound' by the poet William Wordsworth. That of course was before the days of the railway. 'Awe-inspiring' would be a better description of the sound made by 'Black Five' No 45358 and K2 2-6-0 No 61785 as they storm up Glen Falloch towards Crianlarich with the 3.46 p.m. in August 1953.   [C. Lawson Kerr]

The prototype K4 2-6-0, No.3441 *Loch Long*, carrying its later LNER number (1993) climbing Glen Falloch. *Loch Long*, designed by Sir Nigel Gresley especially for the West Highland, emerged from Darlington Works in 1937 and was soon followed by a further five to a similar design. When this photograph was taken, No.1993 was obviously suffering from years of hard work and neglect during the war. [C. Lawson Kerr]

B1 No.61325, newly outshopped in apple green livery and bearing on its tender the full name of its new owner, British Railways, near Inverarnan with the 3.46 p.m. in June 1948. This small hamlet at the south end of Glen Falloch, lies at the border of Dunbartonshire and Perthshire. Loch Lomond steamers came as far as Inverarnan before Ardlui pier was opened, and the inn was used by the engineers during the construction of the railway. [C. Lawson Kerr]

K1 2-6-0 No.61997
MacCailin Mor
descends Glen Falloch
with a Mallaig to
Glasgow train in June
1953.

[C. Lawson Kerr]

40

One of the K4 2-6-0s just introduced to the West Highland, No.3444 *Lord of the Isles,* photographed leaving Crianlarich with the 3.49 p.m. to Glasgow in July 1939.
[C. Lawson Kerr]

The Loch Sloy hydro-electric scheme at Inveruglas required special trains to be operated to take the workmen, both civilians and prisoners-of-war from Faslane, to and from the site. Special platforms were constructed at Glen Falloch, Inveruglas and Faslane. This rare photograph taken in May 1947 shows K3 2-6-0 No.1855—a class not normally associated with the West Highland, and one of the few members of the class with a Great Northern tender—shunting the workmen's train, consisting of vintage North British rolling stock, at Crianlarich.

[C. Lawson Kerr]

One of the un-named K2 2-6-0s, No.61786, being turned in beautiful surroundings at Crianlarich, prior to piloting an excursion back to Glasgow on·20 June 1959. Crianlarich shed was used for storing redundant D11 4-4-0s during the early 1960s, and still stands.

[W. A. C. Smith]

A pair of 'Glens' waiting for departure time from Crianlarich with a southbound train in 1938. D34s Nos.9494 *Glen Loy* and 9242 *Glen Mamie* have taken water at the two water towers provided at Crianlarich for double-headed trains. [C. Lawson Kerr]

The connecting spur between the Callander & Oban and West Highland lines at Crianlarich was not used for regular passenger services until the closure of the Dunblane-Crianlarich section, although it had been in existence since the turn of the century. It was used, however, for excursion traffic, as on 20 June 1959, when K2 No.61786 and B1 No.61261 were photographed climbing up from the Callander & Oban line with the 1.45 p.m. Television Train from Glasgow (Buchanan Street), returning to Queen Street—outwards via Callander and returning via Ardlui. The Television Train was equipped with a television studio, and broadcasts describing the area passed through could be made to the passengers via screens erected above the vestibule doors in the coaches. This circular tour was very popular and, known as the 'Six Lochs Land Cruise', was latterly operated by diesel multiple units. In steam days reversal was necessary at Crianlarich (see page 45). [W. A. C. Smith]

The West Highland line crosses the Callander & Oban at Crianlarich on a girder bridge. Standard Class 5 No.73078 and B1 No.61140 drift into the Upper station with an afternoon train from Mallaig on 8 August 1959. The Callander & Oban at this point is now closed to passenger traffic, but is still used by special timber trains between Crianlarich and the pulp mill at Corpach. [H. Stevenson]

This old coach body on the platform at the isolated crossing loop at Gorton was used as a school for children from the surrounding area and formed one of the most unusual schools in the country. The entire railway staff are seen on the platform. The loop divided the sixteen mile-section between Bridge of Orchy and Rannoch, being one of the first to be operated with tokenless block instruments, allowing it to be switched out. Eventually it became impossible to find staff for this lonely outpost, and the signal box and platform have been razed to the ground. [J. Kernahan]

On a wet day in August 1957, LMS Class 5 No.44908 pilots
K2 No.61774 *Loch Garry* out of Spean Bridge with the
morning train to Fort William. Spean Bridge's third signal
box can be seen in the background, while the Invergarry
and Fort Augustus booking office, now used as a post
office, is situated behind the bush on the up platform.
[C. Lawson Kerr]

During the construction of the West Highland, the company ran into financial straits, principally due to the unexpected difficulties encountered in the construction of the
line over Rannoch Moor, and one of the directors, J. H.
Renton, gave a part of his private fortune to enable construction of the line to proceed. The navvies involved in
the work sculptured this fine image of Renton, which still
stands at Rannoch station. [J. Kernahan]

Ben Doran dominates the Horse Shoe Curve between Tyndrum and Bridge of Orchy, the railway at this point clinging to the lower slope of three mountains in a wide 'U' formation rather than crossing a wide valley on a costly viaduct. K2 No.61793 passes under Ben Doran with the morning West Highland goods on a fine day in April 1961. Ben Odhar (2948') can be seen in the background.
[C. Lawson Kerr]

J36 0-6-0 No.65313, acting as station pilot, pulls a rake of coaches out of the old station at Fort William. The station and signal box have now been demolished, and a new station constructed further away from the town centre due to a road improvement scheme. Below K4 2-6-0 No.61995 *Cameron of Lochiel* at the old Fort William station after working a railtour from Glasgow on 18 June 1960. [W. A. C. Smith]

Shunting the lengthy West Highland trains within the cramped confines of Fort William station was always awkward. A Sunday excursion from Bridgeton on 5 September 1954 was worked by two 'Black Fives', Nos.44921 and 44973. The ornate station building has now gone in the road improvement scheme.   [W. A. C. Smith]

The Mallaig Junction signal—one of the last NBR lower quadrant signals on the West Highland. The new Fort William station is now controlled from Mallaig Junction signal box.   [J. Kernahan]

A fine portrait of a 'Glen' at Fort William shed in late LNER days—No.2474 *Glen Croe*, photographed in September 1947. By this date the 'Glens' had been replaced on most passenger turns by the more powerful 'Lochs' and K4s, and *Glen Croe* is carrying the headcode for a freight working.

[C. Lawson Kerr]

The original West Highland Railway included a branch from Fort William to a station at Banavie, providing connections with Caledonian Canal steamers. The Mallaig extension therefore commenced from this branch at Banavie Junction, a simple single line junction with no crossing facilities. Note the distant signal for Banavie Swing Bridge box, painted red, and with a straight rather than a chevron white band.

[F. Sherlock]

The Mallaig extension was one of the first lines to make use of concrete for its civil engineering features, and both platforms and station building at Glenfinnan were constructed of this. K2 2-6-0 No.62052 arrives with a freight for Mallaig on 21 July 1958. The driver appears to be offering the tablet to a small boy watching proceedings near the signal box.

[W. A. C. Smith]

The Mallaig extension crosses the Caledonian Canal at Banavie, close to the series of locks known as Neptune's Staircase. As at Banavie Junction, the signal box does not control a crossing loop, but is required for the level crossing and swing bridge over the canal. After the station was unstaffed, it suffered badly from vandalism, and has now been demolished.

[J. Kernahan]

Just out of the shops, immaculate in its last coat of LNER apple green paint, Gresley K2 No.1782 *Loch Eil* basks in brilliant sunshine at Mallaig in September 1947. Originally used on the Great Northern Railway, these engines came to the West Highland line in the 1930s, and for thirty years were worked hard in this mountainous territory, a complete contrast to the flat area of England from which they came.
[C. Lawson Kerr]

Two K2s, Nos.61784 and 61764 *Loch Arkaig,* on the climb out of Glenfinnan with the heavy 5.15 a.m. from Glasgow to Mallaig on 21 July 1958. Note the meat vans behind the engines.

[W. A. C. Smith]

One of the crossing loops lengthened to accommodate additional wartime traffic was Lochailort, but rationalisation has meant that this loop is now lifted. This picturesque platform, with its neat NBR starting signal, is thus no longer in use.

[J. Kernahan]

Shortly after Nationalisation, K2 2-6-0
No.61787 *Loch Quoich* leaving Mallaig
with a mixed train for Fort William. This
is one of the last lines in Britain on which
mixed trains are still operated.

[J. G. Dewing]

The view from Mallaig Station signal
box, over the Sound of Sleat to the
'Cocktail Islands' (Rhum, Eigg, Canna
and Muck) is possibly the finest from any
signal box in Britain. Those on the
Mallaig extension were designed by the
Railway Signal Company, and were
similar to those used on the Invergarry &
Fort Augustus Railway.   [J. Kernahan]

Probably the most fascinating railway in Scotland was the Invergarry & Fort Augustus. An independent concern, it was opened in 1903, and ran for 24 miles up the Great Glen from Spean Bridge on the West Highland to Fort Augustus at the southern end of Loch Ness. In this photograph of the Fort Augustus terminus taken prior to the opening of the line, the contractor's wagons and locomotive are preparing to set off for the construction site. Note the sailing vessel on the Caledonian Canal.   [J. H. Wright collection]

The line at the outer platform of Fort Augustus station led to the Pier station, this one mile-long track being used for only three years, closing in 1906. This short section was one of the most expensive to construct, involving a swing bridge across the Caledonian Canal, as well as a viaduct (opposite) across the River Oich. The elaborate castellations were more in keeping with a line having too much rather than too little capital.

[J. H. Wright collection]

This view of Fort Augustus station taken from the Caledonian Canal shows the swing bridge across the canal leading from the outer platform. The continuation from the other side of the canal to the Pier station had been long out of use by the date of this photograph, 14 June 1927. The signal box, which had not been constructed at the time of the photograph opposite, can be seen. It is of the same design as that used on the Mallaig extension which was built just before the Invergarry & Fort Augustus.

[H. C. Casserley]

NBR 4-4-2T No.9155 at Fort Augustus on 23 July 1931. The lengthy platforms provided were rather excessive, as one coach was usually sufficient for the traffic; No.9155 is hauling a brake composite with six compartments, which was quite well filled that day. Passenger services were withdrawn within three years of this date. [H. C. Casserley]

After expending its funds on such unnecessary frills as the elaborate piers on the Oich Viaduct, the Invergarry had nothing left with which to buy locomotives or rolling stock, and the line lay out of use while the decision was made as to how it should be operated. It would have appeared obvious that the North British should operate the service, but that company appreciated that to do so would be to throw money away. The Highland Railway, anxious to keep its rival out of the Great Glen even at the cost of operating the branch at a loss, took up the challenge, but found that the outlay was too much and withdrew in 1907. HR 4-4-0T No.54 is seen in one of the dock platforms at Fort Augustus. Note the crossover which was not provided when the line was first built (see page 60).   [C. Lawson Kerr Collection]

The small platform at Invergloy served nearby Invergloy House. It opened in 1904, one year after the line opened throughout, and was officially closed by 1914 when this photograph was taken from a passing train.   [F. Sherlock]

The first of the intermediate stations on the Invergarry & Fort Augustus Railway south of Fort Augustus was Aberchalder, which was unusual in that it had an unsignalled crossing loop. A lever frame was operated by the key token for the section. This fine station served a settlement of some six houses. Note the concrete construction of the platform, similar to the Mallaig extension and the Callander & Oban's Ballachulish branch which were all built concurrently. [F. Sherlock]

The north end of the platform at Invergarry, showing the water crane and Loch Oich in the background. The station was over three miles from the village it served, on the opposite side of the loch. [H. C. Casserley]

Gairlochy, the first station on the branch after leaving Spean Bridge. The small signal box can be seen on the platform behind the station building. The line was well signalled, and the longest section, twelve miles between Gairlochy and Invergarry, was split by a crossing loop and signal box at Letterfinlay, the summit of the line on the east bank of Loch Lochy, although it was never brought into use. [F. Sherlock]

Like the Invergarry & Fort Augustus, the Callander & Oban Railway's branch from Connel Ferry to Ballachulish was opened in 1903, but it had a more successful history, not closing until 1966. Caledonian 0-4-4 tanks operated the line for most of its life, and No.55187 is seen outside its shed at Ballachulish.

[C. Lawson Kerr]

A station of particularly unusual design was Ballachulish Ferry, situated near the ferry across Loch Leven, now replaced by a bridge. CR 0-4-4T No.55208 pauses at the station with the afternoon train for Oban on 26 May 1958.
[W. A. C. Smith]

CR 0-4-4T No.55195 waits for custom at Ballachulish with the 3.55 p.m. for Oban on 19 July 1954. The famous slate quarries dominate all photographs of Ballachulish station.   [W. A. C. Smith]

For a short period during the early 1960s, between the withdrawal of the 0-4-4 tanks and the coming of diesels, the Ballachulish branch was operated by Ivatt 2MT 2-6-0s. One of these, No.46460, is seen here at Appin.

[G. N. Turnbull]

Sizable station buildings, and large—almost out of proportion—signal boxes, characterised the Ballachulish branch. Tablet instruments were housed in the station buildings at Kentallen and Benderloch, and in addition Kentallen (left) boasted a tea room.

[J. Kernahan]

The Ballachulish branch crossed Loch Etive by the Connel Bridge, the second largest span in Britain. The crossing of the bridge by road vehicles was a permanent problem from the date of the line's opening until its closure, when tolls were abolished and the bridge adapted solely for road traffic; a narrow roadway had been provided in railway days, as can be seen in this photograph of 0-4-4-T No.55224 coming off the bridge with a train from Ballachulish on 14 May 1960.

[W. A. C. Smith]

For a period the Caledonian Railway operated an early form of 'Motorail' service over the bridge, utilising a charabanc formerly used between Clarkston station and Eaglesham, converted to run on rails, and hauling a wagon on which a car could be carried. [J. Kernahan collection]

Stanier 'Black Five' No.44960 rests in the summer evening sun at Oban in July 1962, shortly before the withdrawal of steam on the Callander & Oban. The bay platforms, outside the main building, were constructed in 1903 at the time of the opening of the Ballachulish branch.

[C. Lawson Kerr]

Caledonian Railway
'Oban Bogie' 55 Class
No.14604 and
Highland Railway
'Clan' No.14769 *Clan
Cameron* arriving at
Oban in 1937.
[C. Lawson Kerr]

Two of McIntosh's
'Oban Bogies',
Caledonian 55 Class
Nos.14601 and 14605
preparing to leave
Oban in 1928. Nine
locomotives of this
class were built in 1902
and 1905, designed
especially for the
curves and gradients
of the Callander &
Oban line.
[C. Lawson Kerr]

Stanier Class 5 No.45475 sets off from Oban with an evening express for the south in the summer of 1962. At this date the train conveyed a restaurant car and through sleeping car to Euston. [C. Lawson Kerr]

On 12 May 1962 the two restored pre-Grouping Scottish locomotives, CR 4-2-2 No.123 and NBR 'Glen' No.256 *Glen Douglas* visited Oban with a special excursion from Glasgow. Both are seen here in these two views on the Oban turntable. Note the beautifully etched thistles on No.123's buffers. To keep these in pristine condition this locomotive was always the pilot when doubleheading, and never ran tender first.
[C. Lawson Kerr]

One of the Ivatt 2-6-0s imported to the area to work the Ballachulish branch, No.46468, with a short train of oil tanks at Oban Goods Junction. The express passenger head-code, very rarely seen on the Callander & Oban, seems to be particularly inappropriate in this case.

[C. Lawson Kerr]

The Highland Railway built eight powerful 4-6-0s, the 'Clan' class, and when the Stanier 'Black Fives' arrived on the HR main lines, the 'Clans' found themselves working on the Callander & Oban. No.14765 *Clan Stewart,* which had been temporarily converted to an oil burner in 1920, is seen leaving Oban with the 6.25 p.m. to Glasgow (Buchanan Street) in August 1938. [C. Lawson Kerr]

By 1939, the Stanier Class 5s had begun to make their appearance on the Oban road, and the brief five year reign of the Highland 'Clans' was over. No.5081 is descending the bank into Oban with an express from the south in August 1939. [C. Lawson Kerr]

An unusual visitor to Oban on 14 May 1960 was restored Great North of Scotland D40 No.49 *Gordon Highlander* with a railtour, consisting of the two preserved Caledonian coaches (which can now be seen at the Society's depot at Falkirk) and an observation car. The train is seen here on the return journey, passing the Glencruitten up distant signal, a fine example of a Caledonian lower quadrant.

[C. Lawson Kerr]

A lightly-loaded train, hauled by B R Standard Class 5 4-6-0 No.73120, climbs the last few yards to the 300′ summit at Glencruitten with a southbound train from Oban in July 1962.   [C. Lawson Kerr]

Class 5 No.45153 arriving at Connel Ferry with the 8 a.m. from Glasgow (Buchanan Street) to Oban on 19 July 1954. Connel Ferry could be a station of substantial activity at certain times of the day. The spur to allow through running from Oban to Ballachulish was never completed, and trains for the branch had to run round here. At mid-day, however, the branch train dispensed with the six mile trip to Oban, connections being provided by through main line trains. The branch train can be seen enjoying its 35 minute rest in the main line platform.   [W. A. C. Smith]

When the Callander & Oban line was opened to Oban in 1880 the final six miles from Connel Ferry was one section, and delays became common due to the time taken to climb the 1 in 50 gradients from both Oban and Connel Ferry to the summit at Glencruitten. The additional traffic to the Ballachulish branch which was due to open shortly resulted in an additional signal box and crossing loop being opened at Glencruitten on 9 October 1901. One of the most unusual signal boxes in the country, it consisted of a large Gothic type house, with the lever frame and tablet instruments in a front room. The loop was closed in May 1966.   [J. Kernahan]

The excursion worked by G N S R 4-4-0 No.49 *Gordon Highlander* is seen again, this time in the Pass of Brander, with the waters of Loch Awe in the background. The train is passing 'Anderson's Piano', the system of safety wire fencing invented by the Callander & Oban Secretary, John Anderson, and so called because of the musical effect caused by their vibration in the wind. The steep hillside at this point is studded with boulders which may at any time fall on the line. Should one fall and break the wire fence the signals automatically go to danger, and alarm bells sound in adjacent surfacemen's cottages. The fence is positioned in such a way that if a boulder clears the fence it will not land on the railway. In addition to the stone-warning signals, the post in the photograph carries the Awe Crossing down distant.

[W. A. C. Smith]

The long sections between stations on the Callander & Oban required crossing loops to be established in isolated spots. To provide accommodation for the staff, the signal box was built with a house attached, bell signals being repeated in the house. There were six of these buildings on the Caledonian system, five of them between Dunblane and Oban. Awe Crossing, between Taynuilt and Loch Awe, was opened in 1893, at the same time as the nearby halt at Falls of Cruachan.   [J. Kernahan]

The Caledonian Railway had
244 Drummond 'Jumbo'
0 6 0s, built between 1000
and 1897, but it was not until
the 1930s that these engines
found themselves on
passenger duties on the
Callander & Oban. The last
design of the Highland
Railway was Cumming's
'Clan' 4-6-0, which also were
first seen on the C&O in the
1930s. 'Jumbo' No.17463
pilots No.14763 *Clan Fraser*
into Loch Awe station in
August 1937.   Below,
Restored veterans CR
No.123 and NBR No.256
Glen Douglas approaching
Loch Awe with an excursion
from Glasgow on 12 May
1962.   [C. Lawson Kerr]

Stanier Class 5 4-6-0 No.45049 in Glenlochy with a freight in June 1962, a short time before the end of steam on the Callander & Oban and West Highland lines.   [C. Lawson Kerr]

The twelve mile section between Tyndrum Lower and Dalmally was broken by a combined house and signal box at Glenlochy Crossing. Note the slightly different design to Awe Crossing (page 78). Both loops closed in 1966.

[J. Kernahan]

Crianlarich East Junction with the connecting spur to Crianlarich Upper on the West Highland on the right of the photograph (see page 47). The viaduct carrying the West Highland line to Fort William over the River Fillan can be seen in the background. The 5.15 p.m. from Oban takes the Callander line on 20 July 1957. The 'Beaver Tail' observation car was one of two originally built for the L N E R streamlined 'Coronation Scot' between Kings Cross and Edinburgh. These latterly were used on the West Highland and Callander & Oban lines, but were rebuilt around 1960 to give improved viewing from the rear window. Both are now preserved. [W. A. C. Smith]

Two views of
Drummond 'Jumbos'
in July 1938: No.17401
pilots Highland 'Clan'
4-6-0 No.14769 *Clan
Cameron* with an
express from Oban at
Crianlarich Lower.
Below, No.17423
shunts a west bound
pick up goods at Luib.
Note the unusual
design of signal box.
[C. Lawson Kerr]

Stanier Class 5 No.45158 *Glasgow Yeomanry* drifting down from Glenoglehead to Balquhidder with the 12.56 p.m. from Oban to Buchanan Street on 2 January 1962. From near this point, the view looking eastward over Loch Earn was reputedly the finest view available from a train anywhere in Britain.

[W. S. Sellar]

Two 'Black Fives', Nos.44967 and 44702, taking water at Balquhidder while working a Television Train excursion from Glasgow (Buchanan Street) to Oban on 26 May 1958. Balquhidder was the junction for the line along the north bank of Loch Earn to St Fillans and Crieff, but when the Dunblane-Crianlarich section closed in 1965 both Balquhidder's signal boxes were closed and the station, once used as a church for the local inhabitants, was an unstaffed halt.

[W. A. C. Smith]

CR No.123 and NBR No.256 *Glen Douglas* pause at Glenoglehead crossing with a special in May 1962. The summit of the Callander & Oban Railway, it was the original station for Killin until the village's own railway opened in 1886. For the first three years of the C&O this isolated spot was the railway's western terminus. It was near here that a landslide caused the line's permanent closure in September 1965, a few weeks prior to the official closure date.
[W. S. Sellar]

Caledonian 0-4-4T No.55222 at Killin on 6 August 1957 with the one coach train for Killin Junction exchange platform. It was a steep climb at 1 in 50 for the four mile trip and locomotives normally faced the gradient. There was no loop at Killin, and gravity shunting was used instead of running round. [W. S. Sellar]

The Killin Railway actually terminated at Loch Tay station, although the latter closed in September 1939. The branch engine continued to use the small running shed, and the station was visited by the 'Scottish Rambler' excursion, worked by BR 2-6-4T No.80093, on 12 April 1963. The distinctive station building, by this time used as a private house, was of a design similar to that used on the Balerno branch near Edinburgh.

[W. A. C. Smith]

The only diesels on the Killin Railway were the multiple units which made occasional visits with the 'Six Lochs Land Cruises' in the 1960s. For the last four years of the line's existence BR Standard 2-6-4Ts were used, and No.80092 is seen here with the 1.42 p.m. from Killin, a mixed train, on 12 May 1962. This type of train can now be seen again as engine, coach and wagons are all represented in the Scottish Railway Preservation Society collection.

[W. S. Sellar]

The 'Beaver Tail' observation car at the rear of a train from Oban at Killin Junction on 6 August 1957. The line to Killin drops down behind the signal box.

[W. S. Sellar]

Of the 842 Stanier 'Black Fives' found all over the LMS system, only four were endowed with nameplates. One of these privileged locomotives, No.45157 *The Glasgow Highlander,* is seen approaching Strathyre with a relief for Oban on 12 August 1961.

[W. A. C. Smith]

Strathyre station, looking north. The original building was destroyed by fire in 1893. The beautiful fountain, in the shape of a heron carved out of granite, is still on the Callander & Oban, having been moved to Dalmally when Strathyre closed in 1965.

[W. A. C. Smith]

e of the BR Standard Class 5 4-6-0s with Caprotti valve gear, No.73147, passing the small platform at
ig-na-Cailleach between Callander and Strathyre, with a down freight on 12 August 1961. Trains
led here once a week to take surfacemen's wives on shopping excursions. There were two automatic
ne signals (see page 78) near Craig-na-Cailleach plus a special bell and telephone in the cottage which
be seen in this photograph, for communication with the station master at Strathyre in the event of a
kfall.   [W. A. C. Smith]

Stanier Class 5 No.45214 skirting Loch Lubnaig with the 12.45 p.m. Oban to Edinburgh (Princes Street) on 12 August
1961. The beautiful condition of the ballast and track in this section regularly won prizes for the Craig-na-Cailleach
gangers, and a large sign indicating that this was a 'Prize Length' was exhibited near St Brides.   [W. A. C. Smith]

LMS Class 5 No.45099, with an Oban to Glasgow train on 6 August 1957, approaching the Falls of Leny, near the site of St Brides crossing, which closed on 23 September 1951. Loch Lubnaig lies between the hills in the background. On the hill on the east side of the loch is a watch tower used by the Forestry Commission.

[W. S. Sellar]

Two 'Black Fives', Nos.45319 and 45153, approaching Callander West signal box with the 9.30 a.m. from Oban to Glasgow on 12 August 1961. The signalman is waiting to accept the tablet for the section from Strathyre. The Callander & Oban was single track throughout, except for double track sections between the East and West signal boxes at the junctions at Connel Ferry, Crianlarich, Killin Junction, and Balquhidder. The section from Callander West to Callander & Oban Junction, where the C & O made an end-on junction with the Dunblane Doune & Callander Railway, was also double, until the closure of Callander & Oban Junction signal box in April 1938. After this date, the double section at Callander lay only between East and West boxes.

[W. A. C. Smith]

A busy scene at Callander station on 30 March 1959. A 'Six Lochs Land Cruise' crosses with the 9.18 a.m. from Oban to Glasgow, worked by LMS Class 5 No.45153; another Class 5, No.45213, sits in the background with an up freight. This fine station has now been demolished, and the site is used as a car park.   [W. A. C. Smith]

An illegal visitor to Callander; V2 2-6-2s were not authorised to work west of Dunblane, so the appearance of No.60818 on the 12 noon to Stirling on 23 May 1964 was completely unexpected. [W. S. Sellar]

Two Caledonian 'Dunalastair III' 4-4-0s working tender to tender at Callander in the 1930s. The leading locomotive is No.14348. None of the 'Dunalastair III's survived to become part of British Railways stock. Note the footbridge with the clock tower which, being destroyed in an accident, was replaced with the simpler structure seen in the upper illustration. [E. E. Smith]

Less than two months before the closure of the line, LMS Class 5 No.45359 passes through Drumvaich loop, between Callander and Doune, with the 1.18 p.m. from Callander to Glasgow on 11 September 1965.

[W. A. C. Smith]

The exterior of Doune station, showing an engine of rather obscure origin cut in the ivy.

[J. Kernahan]